The Ultimate Pay-Per-Click Guidebook

A Peak into PPC

AMARPREET SINGH

Publisher - The Thought Flame

THE THOUGHT FLAME
TURNING SPARK INTO FLAME

info@thethoughtflame.com

www.thethoughtflame.com

Table of Contents

Introduction

There are many different ways that you can advertise your affiliate marketing business to gain more traffic and more followers. Some of the ways that you have probably comes across may have included marketing on social media networks, forum marketing or even CPA marketing.

In this eBook you will learn how to leverage PPC advertising campaigns to jump start your affiliate marketing business and learn how to use PPC to drive tons of traffic to your sales page or website. You will also learn how to make the most out of your PPC campaign without losing money in the process.

So, what are you waiting for? Let's get started.

Chapter One: The Basics of PPC Advertising

If you have never heard of PPC marketing before or have heard about it, but wish to know more, this is certainly the perfect eBook for you. In order to fully understand the power of PPC advertising, you need to understand the basics of it all first.

So, what is PPC? PPC simply stand for Pay-Per-Click and it is the process in which an advertiser will pay a small fee each time one of their ads is clicked upon. Pretty much look at it as you paying for visitors rather than scrounging around for them. It is one of the most popular ways to advertise a business today and it is used by millions of people worldwide.

There are many different types of PPC advertising campaigns available online today such as Yahoo Ads and Bing Ads, but the most popular type of PPC campaign used today is Google AdWords.

about 8,220,000 results (0.48 seconds)

PPC Ads

Dog Food Advisor: Dog Food Reviews and Ratings
www.dogfoodadvisor.com/ ▾
The Dog Food Advisor's unbiased **dog food reviews** and dog food ratings searchable by brand or star rating. Find the best dry, canned or raw food for your dog.
Dog Food Reviews by Brand - Dry Dog Food Reviews - Best Dog Foods - Forums

Dog Food Reviews by Brand
www.dogfoodadvisor.com/dog-food-reviews/brand/ ▾
The Dog Food Advisor's unbiased **dog food reviews** searchable by brand. Get help finding the best dry, canned or raw food for your dog.

Dry Dog Food Reviews | Dog Food Advisor
www.dogfoodadvisor.com/dog-food-reviews/dry/ ▾
For dry **dog food reviews**, please click one of the following links. Bowl of Dry Dog Food · 5-Star Dry Dog Foods · 4-Star Dry Dog Foods · 3-Star Dry Dog Foods ...

Dog Food Reviews - Main Index - Powered by ReviewPost
www.dogfoodanalysis.com/dog_food_reviews/ ▾
6 Star Premium Dry **Food** (5 viewing) Premium **foods** with 6 star rating. 23, 21. 5 Star Premium Dry **Food** (3 viewing) Premium **foods** with 5 star rating. 63, 63 ...

Dog Food Reviews, Ratings and Analysis 2014 - PetFoodTalk
petfoodtalk.com/dogfoodreviews/ ▾
Dog food reviews and ratings to help you find the best for your pet. Featuring 2014 in-depth reviews, analysis of dog food ingredient lists, consumer reviews, dog ...

Best Dog Food - Top 4 Dog Food Reviews
www.consumersearch.com › Family & Pets ▾
...perts agree: There really is a difference between **dog food** brands. Although the best

Compare Dog Food to BLUE
www.bluebuffalo.com/ ▾
4.6 ★★★★☆ rating for bluebuffalo.com
Take the True BLUE Test. See How Your **Dog Food** Compares to BLUE

Choose The Best Dog Food
www.hillspet.com/BestDogFood ▾
Compare Brands & See Why to Feed Your **Dog** Hill's® Ideal Balance™.

Best Dog Food
www.petsmart.com/FoodGuide ▾
4.6 ★★★★☆ rating for petsmart.com
Find the Right **Food** for Your **Dog** at Your Local PetSmart®-Shop Today!

Purina® Pro Plan® Reviews
www.proplan.com/Ratings-And-Reviews ▾
4.4 ★★★★☆ rating for proplan.com
Dog Food Made With Real Meat, Fish Or Poultry. Learn More Today!

Beyond® Natural Dog Food
www.purina.com/BeyondCoupon ▾
4.7 ★★★★☆ rating for purina.com
Save $5 On Beyond® Dry **Dog Food**. Any Size, Any Recipe. Try It Today!

How Does Google AdWords Work?

Google AdWords is considered to be one of the most popular and high ranking PPC advertising system in the entire world. Millions of users worldwide use this system on a daily basis to drive relevant and quality traffic to their sales page or website. This system allows virtually anybody to create an ad and to place it upon Google's own search engine or other properties in order to gain this quality traffic.

But how does it all work?

Well, by using the PPC system, users are able to place a certain bid on a keyword of their choice specifically for their ads and set those ads to go live on Google. Then Google itself digs into the large pool of advertisers to choose a certain amount of winners to appear in the various pages of their search engine. The lucky advertisers that get to appear on the front page of Google are selected based on a variety of different factors such as what their chosen keywords are, their bidding price for that keyword and how many ad campaigns they have running.

This system is implemented in such a way that users are able to pay for advertising that will fit nicely into their own budget. Think of Google AdWords as more of an auction. The more you bid, the more traffic you will earn in return.

You can see how this can be helpful especially in affiliate marketing. As Google is the most popular search engine used today, it gets a ton of traffic on a daily basis and you are able to get a piece of that traffic just by placing an ad on their search engine.

The Importance of Keyword Research In Your PPC Campaign

The only way to make the most out of your PPC campaign, you will need to conduct thorough keyword research beforehand. While I know that keyword research can be very time consuming and bothersome for some, it is still incredibly important. Remember, you cannot have a PPC campaign without good keywords and even the best PPC campaigners continue to grow and refine their list of PPC keywords on a daily basis.

What kind of keywords should your PPC campaign consist of? Well, here is a short list of the optimum keywords your campaign should have.

1. Longtail Keywords-Just as the name implies, long tail keywords are long keywords that you may not even be aware of. An example of a longtail keyword can be something such as "make real money online free" or "seo content writer for hire." These keywords have the ability to drive even more high quality traffic to your sales page or website as they are more specific and are less common than short keywords.

2. Relevant Keywords-if there is one thing that you want to avoid it is paying for traffic that has absolutely nothing to do with what you are promoting. To make sure that you will drive the kind of traffic that you are looking for try to find as many keywords that have a high click through rate specifically for PPC campaigns. Try to bid on keywords that are relevant to what it is you are promoting.

Once you have your long list of relevant, long tail and common keywords ready and you have created a budget that you would like to stick to, you are officially ready to start your first PPC campaign. Remember, as this is going to be your first PPC campaign expect to make a lot of mistakes. As time goes on you will slowly get the hang of your campaign and will work continuously to refine it.

Chapter Two: Setting Up Your First Profitable Google PPC Campaign

Remember, if you are looking to drive tons of traffic to your website or sales page, using Google AdWords is certainly the system that you will want to leverage. However, when you first log into the system your first time you may feel very overwhelmed by what you see. I am here to tell you that it is not as complicated as it may look. Once you get the hang of how to use the system and how to make it work for you, you will be excited to start new campaigns on your own.

Follow this step-by-step guide to using the Google AdWords PPC campaign system and to start your first PPC campaign for your affiliate marketing business.

All online campaigns

| Campaigns | Ad groups | Settings | Ads | Keywords | Audiences | Ad extensions | Dimensions | Display Network | ▾ |

| All but removed campaigns ▾ | | Segment ▾ | Filter ▾ | Columns ▾ | ⬓ | ⬇ | | Search |

| + CAMPAIGN ▾ | | Edit ▾ | Details ▾ | Bid strategy ▾ | Automate ▾ | Labels ▾ |

	Status	Campaign type	Campaign subtype	Clicks	Impr.	CTR	Avg. CPC
▣ **Search Network with Display Select**							
Best opportunity to reach the most customers							
▣ **Search Network only**							
Google search and search partners	Paused	Search Network only	All features	40	10,427	0.38%	£0.90
▦ **Display Network only**							
Google's network of partner websites	Paused	Search Network only	All features	0	5	0.00%	£0.00
▢ **Shopping**							
Best way to create Product Listing Ads	Paused	Search Network only	All features	0	39	0.00%	£0.00
Online video							
Garment T Shirt Printing	Paused	Search Network with Display Select	All features	567	229,292	0.25%	£0.43

Step One: Create Your Keyword List

As I said in the previous chapter, your PPC campaign will be all about what keywords you choose to advertise for your affiliate marketing business. This is the one step that will probably take you the most time to complete as you will need to be as thorough with this list as you possibly can. Remember, keep these facts in mind when creating your keyword list:

1. Find Relevant Keyword-make sure that you jot down any keywords that are specifically about your niche or product. This will help ensure that you are getting the exact type of traffic you want and that you are not getting any visitors that are not interested in your niche whatsoever.

2. Don't Forget To Include Longtail Keywords-if you want to drive even more traffic to your sales page or website, you need to make sure that you jot down as many relevant longtail keywords that you find. If you do not include these keywords in your PPC campaign you will miss out on a ton of high quality traffic that you are looking for.

Step Two: Sign Up With A Free Google AdWords Account

This is absolutely free to do and it can be done easily if you just link your existing Gmail account to your new Google AdWords account.

Step Three: Fill Out Account and Payment Info

With Google AdWords you will be paying for the traffic that the system brings to your sales page or website so make sure that you fill out all of the account and payment information correctly and avoid making mistakes. You will not be charged right away from any traffic sent your way. It will take a couple of days so make sure that you have the money already set aside in your bank account.

Step Four: Choose The Type of Campaign You Would Like To Start and Give The Campaign a Name

The first thing you will need to do when starting a brand new Google AdWords campaign is to choose what type of campaign it is going to be. I highly recommend starting with the "Search Network Only" option as it is one of the easiest to set up and will give you the best results. Then give your campaign a name. It does not need to be fancy. Any name will do just fine.

Step Five: Decide Where Exactly Your Ads Will Show

Next you are going to have to choose the specific geographic location you will want your ads to show in. In this section you will be able to choose whether or not you want to target whole countries, local locations and communities, specific states, popular cities or even province in any country.

If that isn't specific enough you can even target specific longitude and latitude coordinates around the world if you prefer. To do this all that you simply have to do is pick the option labeled, "Let Me Choose."

Step Six: Set Your Daily Budget Limit and Choose Your Specific Bid Strategy

This is where you will need to finally set up how much money you are willing to spend on a daily basis for the ads you will put up on Google. In this section you will need to change the default setting to the option, "Manually Set My Bid." Changing the setting will give you more control over your campaign and allow you to learn more about how to use AdWords in the process. You can always change this setting later if you wish.

The important thing to remember here is that when you set your maximum budget, it is the only amount that Google will be able to withdraw from your credit card or bank account per day. You can even choose to have Google withdraw money ahead of time if you would prefer to pay for the ads before they even show.

It is important that you set your spending budget ahead of time to a specific amount so that you don't check your account one day and find it completely empty of money. Remember, it is completely up to you how much you want to spend on your ads per day. You can rest assured that if you ever plan to do so, you can raise the daily limit sometime down the line.

Step Seven: Write Your First As Within Your First Ad Group

This is the section where you will need to concentrate the most. When it comes to writing your ad there are a few key points that you will need to consider:

- Most people tend to click on ads that contain the keyword they are searching for in the headline.
- Ads that are more appealing to the eye tend to be clicked on more.

In terms of your ad you are generally very limited to a certain number of characters per line. Try not to spend too much time coming up with an ad that will convert better. The more ads you create the more you can play around with which ads convert better for you and the more of those ads you can create later on.

This is the basic version of what your ad will look like upon completion:

- Ad Headline: About 25 Characters Long
- Second Line: About 35 Characters Long
- Third Line: About 35 Characters Long
- Fourth Line: Your URL That Will Be Displayed

Step Eight: Fill Out Which Keywords You Want To Target

Remember that long list of keywords you created in the first place? Well, this is when you will plug in those keywords now and see exactly what kind of results you will get with them in the search engine. It is important that when you paste in your list of keywords that you place either quotes around them, a plus sign or a bracket to get the most results for them.

If there is one thing that I do not recommend you do is dump a list of over a thousand keywords into this section. It will be too many keywords for the ad to target and you may not get the results you are looking for. Try to start with just a handful of keywords for your first ad and work slowly from there.

Step Nine: Set Up Your Maximum CPC (Cost-Per-Click)

This is the step where you will need set up how much you are willing to pay every time someone clicks on your ad for the keyword it will show for. It is important for you to remember that every keyword you put in will cost differently and there overall cost will depend on the parameters Google has set for them. Some of the most common keywords that you will use will have prices of their own.

That is why it is my recommendation that you try to bid on keywords that cost less. Doing this will allow your ad to be seen by as many people as possible instead of spending too much money on high competition keywords that may not be seen by anybody.

Step Ten: Review All Of The Information That You Set Up

Before you actually put your ads up and start running them, you will want to double-check everything you have set up. Double check your CPC and daily budget to make sure you will be paying only the prices you want and that your ads will show on the specific pages that you want.

Step Eleven: Confirm Your Payment Information and Run Your Ads

Before you can even start running your ads, you will need to make sure that you have entered your payment information correctly and that it has been confirmed by Google. Once it has, your ads will start running immediately and you can start gaining high quality traffic to your sales page or website.

Chapter Three: Some Helpful Tips To Running a High Converting Ad Campaign

Now that you know how to set up your first every Google AdWords campaign and know how to create your first ad, now it is time to learn how to create ads that will give you the clicks that you are looking for. There are thousands of Google ads that are currently running right now and that are converting as we speak. But how are they doing so well? What is the secret to their success?

In this chapter you will learn a few helpful tips and tricks to create ads that will get the clicks that you are seeking and that will help you get the sales you have been looking for.

High Converting Google Ads

1. Logo Design Ad

Logo Design ® *SALE* $49
www.logodesignguarantee.com/Logo-USA
100% Custom-Made + Special USA Sale
100% Money Back. Order Online Now..

With this ad design, you may first look at it and just automatically assume that it looks like any ad that you will see upon Google. However, there are a few reasons as to why this ad would convert much better than any other ad currently on Google for the keyword of its choice.

- **It's Use of Numbers-**Most Google ads that use numbers tend to be more successful in their campaigns then those that do not use numbers. In this case the number $49 really does stand out as well as the "100% Money Back" guarantee.

This allows people who see the ads to actually see what it is they are getting. It also helps to reduce any clicks that are just considered a complete waste of time.

- **The Use of ASCII Characters-**I have personally never seen an ad use more ASCII characters (trademark sign, percent sign and plus sign) before than this one. These characters help make the ad stand out from the competition and will help draw more attention to it.

- **Includes A Call To Action-**this ad lets people know exactly what it is they are supposed to do. With the logo design this ad lets customers know without directly telling them that they should order online from them...right now.

2. Now Hiring

Make $7487 a month?
www.pochiring.com/Work
Find Out How this American Mom
Makes $7,847 a month From Home.

This is a great example to show especially for those that are looking to recruit others into their own home business. Here are a few reasons as to why this ad really stands out above the competition.

- **It Tells A Story-**Right in the first line of the ad, this ad begins to draw in the attention of potential customers by enticing them into a story that they will not be able to resist. This will give the ad a higher click through rate then any other ads currently listed on Google.
- **Its Use of Number-**With the other example we already discussed the

advantage of using numbers. This ad goes above and beyond that by giving the specific number of $7, 487. When you use a specific number you will give a higher level of credibility, which is a factor that is important to have.

- **Added Benefit**-when it comes to marketing in the work from home niche, your competition is very high, making it extremely hard to stand out. However, this ad goes above and beyond by implying if the American mom can make this much money, so can you.

3. 1-800 Help Line

Injured in an **Accident**?
www.1800needhelp.com/
You May Be Entitled to $10,000 +
Free Case Evaluation. 24/7 Call Us

This example is geared towards those who already have access to a 1-800 number such as attorney office, dentist office, insurance companies and other services. Here are a few reasons why this ad stands out above the competition.

- **The Headline-**the headline used in this ad is attention grabbing. While it may not seem like much this headline is used in such a way that it targets a specific audience right off of the bat.

- **Its Use of Numbers-**In the case of this ad, the number that is used, "$10,000 or more" is used in such a way that it will immediately grab the attention of the customers who see it. This will help this ad to generate more clicks in the long run than ads that do not use numbers.

- **The Use of The Word Free-**you would be surprised how much pull the word "Free" has in the online world. This word will not only help your ad to get noticed, but will get the clicks that you want to get on a daily basis. However, this could have a negative impact on your campaign as you may get a couple of clicks from people who are simply looking for a handout.

Conclusion

If you are looking to get more high quality traffic to your sales page or website for your affiliate program, there is no better way to do so then using a PPC campaign. Of course there are different kinds of PPC campaign systems out there to choose from such as Yahoo ads or Bing ads, but the most popular and successful PPC ad around is Google AdWords.

Just like with any system out there, it will take time to get a handle on Google Adwords but hopefully with this guide you will be able to create your own successful PPC ad campaign and even pick up on some helpful tips and tricks to making high converting ads to help boost your sales.

About Us

The Thought Flame is committed to add value to its customers through various books, online courses and other resources. You can learn more about us and our books at www.thethoughtflame.com.

Don't forget to check out our amazing **online video courses** at www.thethoughtflame.com/courses/ to take your knowledge to another level.

To check out our **extraordinary collection of diet/cookbooks**, visit http://www.thethoughtflame.com/category/non-fictional/cookbooks/ .

As a part of our valued relationship with our customers, we keep providing you free promotional books, courses and other stuff on subscribing with us on our site. We have a strict anti-spam policy and assure you no spam mails will be sent to your mailbox.

To subscribe with us, visit www.thethoughtflame.com.

Like our work and would like to say thanks?

Buy us a cup of coffee at www.thethoughtflame.com/coffee/

Author

Amarpreet Singh is an avid learner and his passion for education has made him travel, work and study all across the world. He holds three masters degrees, including MBA, from top universities in Asia.

He is author of dozens of books, many of which are Amazon's bestseller, varying in various topics and categories. He also teaches many online courses having thousands of students across the world.

He has a keen interest in international affairs, economics, global poverty and politics, financial markets and entrepreneurship, and strives to be part of a community that shares the same passion.

He has worked as consultant with organizations like Airbus and The World Bank. He loves travelling and learning about new cultures, and has been fortunate to live/work/travel/study in countries like India, China, Korea, US, South Africa, Japan, Philippines, Singapore, Canada etc., and learn about the culture and lifestyle in each of them. To check out more of his work, visit www.thethoughtflame.com

www.ingramcontent.com/pod-product-compliance
Lightning Source LLC
Chambersburg PA
CBHW030704190526
45164CB00004B/441